Letters from the Underworld

Alan Baker

OPEN HOUSE EDITIONS

Published by Open House Editions 2022
An imprint of Leafe Press
www.leafepresspoetry.com

First published by Red Ceilings Press, England in 2018

ISBN: 978-1-7397213-3-6

Copyright © Alan Baker, 2018 and 2022. All rights reserved.

Cover image : "The Hypocrites" by Gustave Doré
from his illustrations to Dante's "Inferno" (1861)

Acknowledgements:

Some of the letters were published in the following:

Blackbox Manifold
Decals of Desire
The Other Room Anthology 10 (2018)

Letters from the Underworld

1

Thank you for letter; it was good to hear from you. Your words have given me the courage to speak in parables, evoking enhanced images articulating calm. So, send me the city, I'll tuck its suburbs and fold its avenues into the sleep I'm about to fall into; a place to wander spectacularly lost and caring only a little. Marvell wrote about the soul that it preens its wings, perched in a tree. So, slip into the envelope a pressed leaf from The Tree of Lost Causes; that's where my soul, if such a thing exists, might perch and preen. Or, in an alternative version, the tree might bow under the weight of snow, and the suburb be unrecognisable; in fact, it was on such a night that I walked home, late, against the cold wind, and asked myself "Are language and thought the same thing? Is the squawk of a magpie language? Is this sensation of emptiness a kind of knowledge?" Let me know your views.

2

Whose voice she took, I do not know. Whose hand she took, I know; it was mine, for sure, but is that OK? A strange child leading me into the night? Nature is the world's playground, she said, but led me into the town, where people whispered and pointed. The sea lapped at our feet, and she stared out over it and asked "Where are my Mum and Dad"? I'd seek your advice in this matter, but I realise that no-one can teach me how to converse with The Lost People. I have more than one hundred holiday ideas for children, but none for her. Her words are like the howl of a coyote under the desert moon. *Limbus infantium*, for those too young to have committed personal sins. The Magisterium is free to consider this; as it considers, the tideless sea, with its acres of kelp, continues its incessant lament. But that's enough about me. What about your life? Anything dramatic? Does Rumour stalk the land, and, if so, what does she report?

3

Since your last letter I've been living in some kind of altered state, some semblance of life. A series of tyrannies are establishing themselves in the region, and anyone with no home is finding it difficult to get a welcome or drinkable water, or food, or safety. My dreams are increasingly of exile and wandering. That part of the globe lit by the moon wonders at the madness; it smells of leavened bread and encourages people to give themselves up to the night; it is imaginary, of course, and exists only in this letter to you; feel free to make up your own version. How about *"Dusk arranges things to its liking, with diminished colours and sharpened sounds. Something has done its maths, and fractal branches glow in electric light."* That's a good start. We could then add: *"There are no rough sleepers, and no-one is lying awake figuring out how to pay their medical bills. The world turns; there is song, a set of scales and keys; words, a vibration in the mouth and ear; blood, a sense that it no longer rules."* So much for that part of the globe. Here, we avoid our neighbours and watch TV. Are things any different where you are?

4

I've concluded that sincerity is a curse; I see it all around me. Give me tricksters anytime. Tonight I'm feeling lyrical: "Transhumance, ageless and calm, ever drift across the lands; your presence, on the high pastures in spring, or slipping past the gates of detention centres, not caught on camera, keeps us breathing the air of day". These are my passing thoughts. How long can I continue doing this job is another passing thought, frequenting airports, taxis, hotels, wandering emptily and alone round the Old Towns of so many cities. Maybe you could reply to this question, plaintive as it is, but spare me the sincerity. Speak instead in the voices of those refugee families at the Bahnhof, newly-arrived from the south, hoping for Limbo, if not the Elysian Fields; the birch and alder, damp heath with lilies and meadowsweet that surround this outpost where the shops close early and those of limited curiosity are happy. How I envy you the big city, its bleary-eyed insomnia and varieties of shopping experience.

5

I've been travelling a lot; from the forests of the hinterland to this northern archipelago where the daylight lasts till midnight. It's peaceful; the Company is benevolent and there's full employment. But rumours of unrest beyond the borders and land lost to the sea make people uneasy. The streets are tree-lined, with cycle paths and flowerbeds. The doormen look like they're made of Lego. From the harbour wall, I can see little ships send up smoke-rings towards a biplane looping the loop. But it's a tame and threadbare town. The locals say "Go west young man", but I'd say try north-by-north-east; that's where the aspens shed their silver, and birds sing with the voices of children. Don't come here, where negative interest rates threaten stability, and the Foreign Minister attends meetings in a clown's outfit; where the seasons send mixed messages, balmy at midwinter, and the marshes are alive at night with St.Elmo's fire and the calls of what we take to be nocturnal birds. The currency is worthless. Th'hydroptic glass hath never sunk so low.

6

I'd like to be able to see life as an accumulation of kindnesses. I'd like to see sleep as a "companionable silence". But recently, as I think I mentioned in my last letter, the voices in the night returned. They ask me why my eyes are blue and why "threshold" is such a difficult word to pronounce for non-native speakers. One, who has a particularly plaintive lilt, said he paid $3000 in cash, but the boat was just a cheap inflatable. They wanted safety, but the ferryman told them they were already dead; he looked in their mouths for a coin to pay for passage. Those who could pay were rewarded with life in a small, green valley with a post office and cricket pitch, low hills either side, a floodplain with housing stock and gardens inhabited by a strange language in which pauses are instantly filled by News (a fabulous screen of shadowy multiplications, layered facts and laminated happenings). I have to sign off; there's a sheen in the air, rain, or charged ions before rain, before a storm.

7

I decided to walk myself to sleep last night, along a tree-lined boulevard, with voices of children out of sight, trees that seemed to groan and whisper and exhale CO_2 and put out roots to trip me, whose branches were hung with dead mice and small birds. Look at that view! said a voice, and there, through the gap, the city lay below, a tracery of lights. Then I was in a garden. It was sunny and we sat at a little table, with tea and cakes. You were there. We provide a haven here, you said, for those fleeing persecution. But that's not me I said. You smiled, sadly. And who's to say they're not all here, in flashlit splendour, teasingly present with me in this enclosure of sky and rooftop. To call them is natural, but the wind does it for me: shaken world, wide with wanderers displaced and dispossessed, seeking refuge and finding razor wire and shipwreck. But that was last night. Today, walking to the station to go to work, all seems hopeful. The weather reports are kind, and the seas in this region are expected to be calm.

8

A healing ceremony is required. Do you know where I can pick one up cheaply? We are lacking neologisms to delineate our plight. A healing ceremony might help with that. It would be useful, I think, to heal invisible wounds, abstract wounds, unacknowledged wounds, wounds that can't be displayed in the market place; wounds like silver on wisps of sky and rosy-fingered dawn. The multiple lives of the forgotten inhabit my tongue, my eye socket, my nerves and frontal cortex, and engage in feuds with their neighbours. A ceremony might appease them. You probably think I'm taking things too seriously, and should take a few days off, but my tea tastes of jasmine with a hint of abstraction and random numbers, the green of grass is green enough, and cycles and seasons pass and surprise us with their habit of returning. Spring, when miracles cluster in unreasonable abundance; this is what I look forward to.

9

As I write, house martins are circling the eaves, like little perpetual motion machines. When they stop, in a few weeks, summer will unwind. You tell me that it's predominately dry with a fair amount of sunshine; feeling pleasantly warm for most, with another warm day in prospect. It's interesting that it will be turning cloudier later with some showery rain in the south. You tell me that the fine days are endless where you are. Not so here. The aphelion - the point at which Earth is farthest from the Sun, coincides with summer in these hemispheres. In ages past, and, they say, in times to come, the world was at its closest point to the Sun, the perihelion, during our summers. The cave paintings of the Neolithic attest to a warmer, milder climate at this time; the desert was fertile and well-watered. So it may be again. Now, the rocks and sand, with little thermal inertia, alternately bake and freeze by day and night. So, enjoy your temperate zone, and your "sunny intervals"; don't take them for granted.

10

I don't want my words to be sane. Sanity is terrifying! Incensed, I want them incensed. I want their incense to fill my room with its sickly premonitions, its blood-filled laments, its catchy pop-tunes. I don't want my tea to taste of bonded labour and have an existential aroma. Down here, there are no endings or beginnings; circularity rules. You must come and visit. It doesn't take long, though I've heard the journey back can be arduous. Mostly it's impossible. I can be your guide. I can show you the inland sea; it's waterless and covered in a mix of three-bedroomed detached and affordable housing. Seaweed sways at night, and during the day, when everyone's at work, circulatory currents erase all memories. Bluebirds glide over white cliffs. The Central Bank and the IMF insist on shoelessness. There are chariot races every spring. When it was time to leave, I could lead you to the port, but be warned: the ferries are irregular and can't be depended on.

11

I remember something Frank said once: "My feet have never been comfortable". As for me, I want to rest my feet; sit at a cafe in the square, with a glass of the local wine, wearing a pretentious hat and reading a book by Michel Foucault. The circling world would accept me, I'd paint the zero hour into a corner and observe its silence as I sip my wine. I could move with the world, as a Wild Swimmer moves with the current, conserving her energy, relaxed enough to be able to enjoy the play of sunlight and spray on the cliffs, to hear the seabirds cry, to move in harmony with the deep. I could be that swimmer. But I have uncomfortable feet, so I settled down with my book, where I read (I know you're interested in these things), that a quantum processor is operational, but only at a temperature of -260C; if it worked at room temperature, all the cryptology in the world would be rendered useless. No more secrets. Today, nuanced facts bump into rumour and all The City's talking, though no-one wants to listen. Fiscal arrangements shimmer in the rain. The nation doth not know itself.

12

I have a morbid fascination with movement, and an inability to sit still. When darkness falls, this makes me twitchy. I thought last night, for example, that people were calling to me from the past. It was brutal then. They were searching for their relatives. But today I can see that, even as I write, there are people searching for their relatives all over the southern shores. Forgive me, then, if under the circumstances, I want to swim in the River of Forgetfulness. I might remember nothing but morning sun on crags, an earthworm loud in its underground chambers, the creaking of the dry grass, a cell's expansion, splitting and replication. The sea glimpsed between narrow houses is a stranger. Where is the gannet's crash, the dolphin's guile? This, I conclude, could be the end, or an endless series of endings. Anyway, how are you? Things are quiet here. Maybe next time I reach you will be at summer solstice, and its endless varieties of promise will lighten our tone.

13

I wonder whether you think of me often, or at all. Sometimes, in my room of pine floorboards and blue walls with rolling clouds, I wonder whether loneliness is one of life's pleasures, to be refined and cultivated; a connoisseur of solitude I could become, applying social work methods and theories to The Self, applying paste of oak-apples and honey poultices to my wounded soul, which is responsive, in the way that delinquent youths are responsive to the latest advances in behavioural therapy and aromatic remedies based on lavender oil and the resin of certain non-indigenous herbs. Maybe if we all took care of our physical and mental well-being we'd be more inclined to take care of others; maybe there'd be fewer border guards, and the creation of special units to "hunt down" those who slip through the fences into the Forbidden Zone would be seen as a barbaric act. Access to servers containing essential data is difficult to acquire, and anyway, the data is encrypted. The Oracle speaks in riddles. I hope this letter finds you well and manages to get through the firewall.

14

In former times we wandered wide in search of pasture, setting out each morning into the green hills. Such freedom! Do you remember the old footpaths and drover's tracks, when wandering was a pleasure? But the strangers who arrive by night tell a different story; they take detours through underground caverns, follow their GPS through deprived areas of provincial cities, are denied access to places of safety, sleep in bus stations where the stars are erased. I sometimes think that each human life is like a molecular collision, unimaginably small, but affecting everything. The star-clusters climb, Cassiopeia at the zenith, the vast galaxy of Andromeda a smudge on the black expanse. Oh presences, crystalline and cold, lend clarity and care to our sunlit dealings; be counterpoint to and escape from the acts of Day; be the comforting dark in which we sleep. "To see the stars again" said Dante; I know what he means. Bonne soirée. Arrivederci. Good night in every language that you know.

15

In my sleep-deprived state all the people have a kind of beauty, even the guy who tried to scam me on my journey here with the old story about lost luggage. The piped muzak is driving me nuts, but it's inflicted equally on everyone I suppose (though I secretly think that I'm a more sensitive soul than most). Through the observation panels I can see the city raise a lung, suck birds and fountains into its maw, among sirens, hanging gardens, back-streets, exhaust fumes and cheap little factories which provide some kind of hope for the wanderers on foot, carrying children, hungry. The city teems, and vibrates with life, but seems so fragile; vulnerable to plague or pandemic; a tick bite could do it, or a new strain of melancholy brought from the trading posts and ports of the peninsular. They say the seas might rise and cover the earth (they've done it before); they say that in The Book of Cars the Citroen C1 should be praised for fuel economy; they say the man with the furled umbrella sniffs the breeze, as if only he could sense the coming rain.

16

From where I'm sitting, at my writing desk, the cry of the wanderers can be heard from the reserves; some say it is haunting and beautiful, a melody of ancient sorrows; to others, it's an easy lament. The ferry operators say they have to be vigilant against this appeal to shallow, uncomplicated emotions at the expense of reason. They train their telescopes on the distant blue. If only foreign languages had been one of my core competencies I could have interpreted these songs from the Cradle of Civilization and the Great Rift Valley; but the days are getting shorter and the heathland turns brown, then red; a skein of ice on the marsh, portent and harbinger of the change to come. It's nice at this season of the year to have a safe suburban home. Across the flats of the delta the sea stirs in a passionless dawn; could you teach me such calm, such perfect harmony with the world as I know it, or is such stillness lost forever?

17

From your last letter, I take it that you're preoccupied with beachwear and cocktails. All I've got are memories, sidling up and making suggestions out of turn; each one dwelling in a separate zone, kitted out with a biography, a personality and a whole cast of dramatis personae. We dine on melancholy; it's impervious to words, spreading like a sports field on a housing estate on a Sunday afternoon in February; a scene not unlike the view from the lookout posts we are assigned to, watching for forest fires and appreciating the changing colours of the sea and the sun reflecting on the complex channels of the delta. The ultimate is the everyday here. Television is our daily bread. But though melancholy, we have our rages; our leaders encouraged us to throw stones at scarecrows to ease the tension. An epidemic of crows resulted; those lovers of carrion and symbols of the night (though they are, in fact, more intelligent than we give them credit for).

18

Each morning the light through slatted blinds is so unquestioning; as if it were carved in ivory, fixed like an unwavering belief. Nothing wavers much here. Each day, naked people are judged on TV shows; all the pale humans, judged and found wanting. Today my taxi driver was my only interlocutor. *Rivers, mountains, walls and fences are like scars,* he said, *on the map of my life. A fabled country,* he continued, *lay across the river, I've seen it on TV and I've heard its laughter, light and joyful, in dreams and visions; I would like to go there, but since I left my middle years behind I've found that old age is an unforgiving country, a glacial twilight, and once there no satellite navigation system in the world will guide you back. Invisible people, we're invisible here; they look through me as if I were a ghost. The river has widened and the laughter grown faint.*

19

I sometimes feel, when I read your letters, that I could reach out and touch you; the words have your voice, the phrasing the contours of your tongue, the handwriting the morphology of your mental landscape whose valleys I'd like to wander in, perhaps to find a river by whose banks I could fall asleep and dream of the world as an emerald of unreachable beauty, a crystallographer's dream; such a thing is possible, although, as we know, the possible as a dwelling, be it a garden or a sunlit garret, is as mortal as you or I. You wanted to ask me about the secrets I'm privy to? Sure. Ask me any kind of thing. Orchestrate your questions with the breeze's hush in the leaves of the buddleia, butterfly bush, and friend to invertebrates everywhere. Ask me something like: Have you nothing to say about a planet's ruin? Scrawl the meanings with a piece of burnt wood and nail the questions to the wall, why don't you? Answers by return of post, although they may be encrypted.

20

You know me by now, after all this correspondence. I cannot rest from travel. I would drink life to the lees, but instead, I'm stuck here, watching unequal laws being meted and doled unto a savage race (that hoard and sleep and feed, and know not me). This evening, all is calm, here, on this tideless coast. The deep moans round with many voices. The late sun slants into my open window and the lights begin to twinkle from the rocks. The aforementioned voices name cities of men and manners, climates, governments (myself not least... but that's delusion). My government has withdrawn funding from the rescue service and other member states argue amongst themselves while the hungry sea doesn't rust unburnished, but shines in use. This is idle talk, I know. Titanic wasn't built in a day, and the same applies to my plans to get out of here, make a lot of money and quit this crazy scene. The vessel puffs her sail. Any survival tips? But I know I shouldn't ask; you work your work, I mine, and, though much is taken, much abides. But still, I do wonder, if only to myself (made weak by time and fate), exactly what the future holds. It's not too late to seek a newer world, is it?

www.ingramcontent.com/pod-product-compliance
Lightning Source LLC
Chambersburg PA
CBHW071400090426
42736CB00015B/3210